Fallen Angels

A Comedy in Three Acts

by Noël Coward

A SAMUEL FRENCH ACTING EDITION

SAMUEL FRENCH

FOUNDED 1830

New York Hollywood London Toronto

SAMUELFRENCH.COM

ISBN   978-0-573-60880-3   Printed   in   U.S.A.   #431

MUSIC USE NOTE

Licensees are solely responsible for obtaining formal written permission from copyright owners to use copyrighted music in the performance of this play and are strongly cautioned to do so. If no such permission is obtained by the licensee, then the licensee must use only original music that the licensee owns and controls. Licensees are solely responsible and liable for all music clearances and shall indemnify the copyright owners of the play and their licensing agent, Samuel French, Inc., against any costs, expenses, losses and liabilities arising from the use of music by licensees.

IMPORTANT BILLING AND CREDIT REQUIREMENTS

All producers of *FALLEN ANGELS must* give credit to the Author of the Play in all programs distributed in connection with performances of the Play, and in all instances in which the title of the Play appears for the purposes of advertising, publicizing or otherwise exploiting the Play and/or a production. The name of the Author *must* appear on a separate line on which no other name appears, immediately following the title and *must* appear in size of type not less than fifty percent of the size of the title type.

FALLEN ANGELS

CHARACTERS

Julia Sterroll

Fred Sterroll

Saunders

Willy Banbury

Jane Banbury

Maurice Duclos

SCENES

The action of the play takes place in the dining-drawing room of the Sterrolls flat in London.

ACT ONE
Morning.

ACT TWO
Evening.

ACT THREE
The next morning.

Fallen Angels

SCENE: *The dining-room/drawing-room of the Sterrolls' flat in London. Morning. From the audience's point of view there is a large window with a window-seat Up Left, with a baby grand piano below it. Right of the window is the door to the kitchen. Right of this, Up Center, is the inner hall with a writing desk and two chairs. The front door is off Right, out of sight. There is a fireplace on the Right, with the door to JULIA's bedroom below it. Between the fireplace and the hall is a large drinks table or chest for serving drinks from. Right Center is a dining table with two chairs. Left Center is a comfortable couch with a telephone on a table behind it. Over the fireplace there is a mirror. There is another mirror Down Left.*

AT RISE: *When the CURTAIN rises* FRED *is having his breakfast and* JULIA *is sitting in an armchair reading a newspaper and dangling her legs over the arm. She is plainly and appropriately dressed for an ordinary London day in which nothing in particular may be expected to happen. There must not be the faintest suggestion of the usual elegant silks and satins so beloved by the theatrical dressmaker.* FRED *is in golfing clothes.*

JULIA. You'll only get hiccups if you gobble like that.
FRED. I'm not gobbling.
JULIA. What time's Willy coming?
FRED. He ought to be here now.

(*There is a slight pause.*)

5

JULIA. (*Rustling the newspaper.*) I say—Muriel Fen-church is divorcing her husband.

FRED. That's uncommonly generous of him.

JULIA. Do you want any more coffee?

FRED. No thanks, dear.

(*There is another pause.* JULIA *goes on reading.*)

JULIA. (*Reading.*) A girl scout was molested in Gros-venor Square last night.

FRED. Another!

JULIA. Don't be silly, Fred, last time it was a *boy* scout.

FRED. Oh!

JULIA. I think you'd better have some more coffee.

FRED. Why?

JULIA. Because I want you to see our new treasure.

FRED. Oh, all right. I didn't know we had one.

JULIA. She seems a nice girl, but rather grand. (*She rings.*)

FRED. The main thing is that the other one's gone—I couldn't bear her, and I never could remember her name. What was it?

JULIA. Myfanwy.

FRED. Oh. (*He gulps his coffee. Enter* SAUNDERS.) Good morning.

SAUNDERS. Good morning, sir.

FRED. What's your name?

SAUNDERS. Jasmin, sir.

FRED. Oh.

JULIA. We have arranged that she shall be called Saunders.

SAUNDERS. Yes, sir—madam has explained your case to me.

FRED. My case? What case?

SAUNDERS. Your lapses of memory, sir.

FRED. My lapses of memory . . . ? Ah! Oh yes, yes—well, I shan't want any more coffee, Saunders—er—My-fanwy.

SAUNDERS. You're quite right, sir. I was in the employ of His Grace the Duke of Cidarington for three years. His Grace, one of our foremost golfers, as you well know, sir, never took coffee before a day on the course. His Grace always said that it made his hand unsteady.

FRED. Oh! Really?

SAUNDERS. Yes, sir. And since we're on the subject of golf, allow me to congratulate you. I noticed your bag in the hall, and was delighted to see a complete set of Bobby Jones Steel Shafters. I knew at once that you were a connoisseur.

FRED. Thank you very much, Myfanwy—Saunders.

SAUNDERS. May I ask, sir, what balls you use?

FRED. Well—just ordinary balls.

SAUNDERS. His Grace never used anything except Spaldings. And personally I recommend them myself whenever possible. Do you need me for anything else, sir?

FRED. No. Do you want to say anything more?

SAUNDERS. No, I don't think there is anything. Ah, perhaps there is one thing. Which course are you playing on?

FRED. Chichester.

SAUNDERS. Are you taking all your clubs, sir?

FRED. Yes.

SAUNDERS. Oh dear! Surely you must know, sir, your irons are all you need at Chichester. (*Laughing.*) Oh dear! Your irons! Quite sufficient. (*Goes out.*)

JULIA. She seems all right, doesn't she?

FRED. Quite. (*He rises from the table.*) I wish Willy'd learn to be punctual.

JULIA. Shall I ring him up?

FRED. What for?

JULIA. To bring him down.

FRED. It wouldn't do any good. He's most likely in the bath. For him, that's a big job. He does all his thinking in the bath.

JULIA. He should have been down some time ago, then.

FRED. Don't be bitter, dear.

JULIA. Never mind, you've got the whole week-end before you. Two days on Chichester golf course where, according to Saunders, you can only use your irons, should be more than enough.

FRED. Irons, indeed. I'll take the lot.

JULIA. Sit down quietly and smoke.

(FRED *sits in arm-chair.* JULIA *sits on the edge and lights his cigarette.*)

FRED. What are you going to do?

JULIA. Nothing in particular. I shall do my ballet practice . . . (*She does a couple of exercises.*) and tidy up and dust a bit, to set Saunders a good example. I'm lunching with Jane, and we shall probably go to a matinee.

FRED. There now, didn't I tell you your day would pan out normally?

JULIA. Yes, but I did have a presentiment when I first woke up.

FRED. But it was nothing definite, you said so.

JULIA. Of course it wasn't: you can't define a presentiment, that's what's so horrid, the feeling of being unsettled.

FRED. I expect it's indigestion.

JULIA. No, I really felt quite odd, as though something damnable were going to happen.

FRED. If you go on thinking in that vein, something damnable *will* happen.

JULIA. You're being rather taciturn and important this morning.

FRED. I don't like to see you worrying yourself over nothing.

JULIA. (*Laughing.*) I'm not really—I'm very happy.

FRED. Are you—honestly?

JULIA. Of course.

FRED. Sure?

JULIA. Positive!

FRED. Good. I think it's awfully silly of people to lead unhappy lives, don't you?

JULIA. Yes, I suppose so. We shall both know the first minute we go off one another.

FRED. We've been married five years.

JULIA. A divine five years.

FRED. Yes—wonderful!

JULIA. We're not in love a bit now, you know.

FRED. I don't know anything of the sort.

JULIA. It's true.

FRED. The first violent passion is naturally over—

JULIA. Thank God!

FRED. Why?

JULIA. It's so uncomfortable—passion.

FRED. Yes, but it's a thoroughly fundamental thing; one couldn't do without it.

JULIA. You mean we couldn't.

FRED. No, I don't—we could and are doing without it.

JULIA. One can't be really in love without passion, that's why I said we weren't any more.

FRED. Don't be annoying, Julia, you know perfectly well we've reached a remarkable sublime plane of affection and good comradeship, far above—

JULIA. Just ordinary "being in love." I quite agree.

FRED. We *are* in love.

JULIA. Hypocrite—we're not.

FRED. We are—in a different way.

JULIA. There is no different way. It's exactly the same with everybody. I've discussed it with Jane.

FRED. Damn Jane.

JULIA. By all means—but she knows—just as I do.

FRED. You're psycho-analytical neurotics, both of you.

JULIA. That sounds lovely, Fred!

FRED. Do you always discuss everything with Jane?

JULIA. Yes, everything.

FRED. Even the most intimate relationships—us?

JULIA. Yes, you know I do, I always have.

FRED. I think that's dreadful—

JULIA. Nonsense, you discuss everything with Willy.

FRED. Yes, but differently.

JULIA. Less accurately, I expect, that's the only difference.

FRED. I'm sure married life was much easier in Victorian days.

JULIA. If you think women didn't discuss everything minutely in the Victorian days just as much as they do now, you're very much mistaken.

FRED. But it was all so much simpler.

JULIA. For the men.

FRED. For the women, too; they didn't know so much.

JULIA. They didn't give themselves away so much, poor dears, they were too frightened.

FRED. Anyhow, on the whole I'd rather be as we are.

JULIA. That's right, dear.

FRED. But you're wrong when you say I don't love you any more.

JULIA. I didn't say that at all. I know you love me very much and I love you too—you're a darling. But we're not "in love." Can't you see the difference?

FRED. I suppose so, but I don't want to.

JULIA. Well, we won't go on about it any more—you shall go and play golf and quarrel with Willy, and I'll stay at home and quarrel with Jane, and we'll all be awfully happy. Are you coming home tomorrow?

FRED. Perhaps tonight, if the weather's bad.

JULIA. Well, you might telephone me and let me know.

FRED. All right.

(*There is the sound of the FRONT DOOR BELL.*)

JULIA. There's Willy.

FRED. I'll let him in and save Jasmin the trouble.

JULIA. Saunders.

FRED. Saunders, then. (*Goes out into the hall, and after a moment ushers in* WILLY, *who is also in golfing clothes and looking very nice in them.*)

WILLY. Good morning, Julia—how are you?

JULIA. I'm feeling grand. Fred and I have just had a psychological romp—it was very stimulating.

FRED. It's depressed me for the day.

WILLY. Jane's been a trifle difficult this morning.

FRED. In what way?

WILLY. She woke up with a presentiment.

FRED. Good Lord!

WILLY. She went on about it all through breakfast.

JULIA. How tactless of her! I at least waited until after breakfast.

WILLY. Have you had one too?

JULIA. Yes, a beast! But don't ask me to explain it, it's quite intangible at present.

FRED. We'd better go, Willy, and leave them to their dreary forebodings. We'll be very hearty and jolly all day, and drink a lot of beer at lunch.

WILLY. The car's downstairs.

FRED. How thoughtful of you not to bring it up!

WILLY. Have you got your clubs?

FRED. They're in the hall. I'm only taking my irons.

WILLY. Why?

FRED. Because Saunders said so.

WILLY. Who on earth is Saunders?

FRED. Never mind.

WILLY. Goodbye, Julia—don't encourage Jane too much, for heaven's sake.

JULIA. Whatever encouragement there is will be mutual—I feel in a particularly heart-to-heart mood to-day.

FRED. Good bye, darling. (*He kisses her.*)

JULIA. Good bye, love—don't forget to telephone. (FRED *and* WILLY *go out amicably.* JULIA *rings the bell on wall and then begins her ballet practice. She hums a little tune, presently crosses to the piano and begins to play the tune.* SAUNDERS *comes in with a tray to clear the breakfast things away.*) Does it feel awful to be in a new place, Saunders?

SAUNDERS. No, ma'am—not particularly.

JULIA. I'm so glad—I'm sure I should be terrified and break everything.

SAUNDERS. It's just getting used to things, ma'am.

JULIA. I hope you're not secretly hurt at our refusing to call you Jasmin?

SAUNDERS. Oh, no, ma'am—I don't mind.

JULIA. It's a sticky name, isn't it—for the house?

SAUNDERS. I've never thought about it much, madam.

JULIA. That's good—then you won't miss it, will you?

SAUNDERS. No, madam.

JULIA. If rather a strange-looking man calls during the morning, will you take him straight to the bathroom?

SAUNDERS. Yes, madam. Shall I run a bath for him?

JULIA. No. He'll be the plumber.

SAUNDERS. Oh! Excuse me, madam. (JULIA *begins to play.* SAUNDERS *continues to clear away. Her attention, however, is not all taken up by her work. She is obviously listening to the tune* JULIA *is playing. Suddenly.*) B flat!

JULIA. (*Surprised.*) What?

SAUNDERS. (*Slightly embarrassed.*) Excuse me, madam. You played B natural. It should be B flat.

JULIA. Oh, you're musical then, Saunders?

SAUNDERS. I was brought up in a convent, madam.

JULIA. Then you're sure it's B flat?

SAUNDERS. Absolutely.

JULIA. (*Goes over the interrupted musical passage.*) You are right, Saunders. It was B flat.

SAUNDERS. Of course. I have an infallible ear. And it's had plenty of practice. For four years I was with Madame Carmen Granado, the celebrated concert pianist. You can't get by me with a wrong note.

JULIA. I realize that.

SAUNDERS. Madame Granado was very sweet to me. She insisted that I used her own piano for practising.

JULIA. Really?

SAUNDERS. She had a Bechstein grand—

JULIA. I'm afraid mine is only a baby grand.

SAUNDERS. Don't let that bother you, madam. Madame Granado was a celebrity, world-famous—I'm used to making the best of things. Your little instrument'll make a nice change.

JULIA. I'm so pleased—

SAUNDERS. Don't give it another thought, madam. (*Sitting at the piano.*) You'll find that it goes like this . . . (*She begins to play and sing lightly.*)

Meme les Anges succombent a l'amour,
C'est pourquoi done je vous en prie—

(*The DOOR BELL rings.*)

Dieu qui arrange les jours et les sejours,
Laisse moi encore une heure de paradis.

(SAUNDERS *takes no notice of the bell and goes on singing. After a little hesitation,* JULIA *goes to answer the door.* SAUNDERS *goes on with the song.*)

Tous mes amours me semblent comme les fleurs,
Leurs parfume restant douces quand meme—

(*The DOOR BELL rings again.*)

Donne moi tes lévres, ton ame, et ton coeur,
Parce que follement je t'aime—je t'aime—
je t'aime!

(JANE *enters in travelling clothes, carrying a suitcase. She looks extremely startled.* SAUNDERS *continues to sing, without noticing her.*)

Je t'aime—je t'aime—je t'aime! . . .

JANE. (*In a stifled voice.*) Stop singing that song!

SAUNDERS. Oh, ma'am, what a fright you gave me.

JULIA. (*Comes back. To* SAUNDERS.) That'll be all, Saunders. (*To* JANE.) Saunders was just practicing. (SAUNDERS *collects her tray and goes out. The* GIRLS *watch her off.*) I say—why on earth are you all dressed up like that?

JANE. (*Back in the mood in which she entered.*) You don't know—that's all—you just don't know.

JULIA. Why, what on earth's the matter?

JANE. And then to come in and find your maid singing *that* song. I should like a glass of water.

JULIA. What nonsense—you've only just finished breakfast.

JANE. We must both go away at once.

JULIA. (*Amiably.*) All right, where shall we go?

JANE. Don't be maddening, Julia, I'm serious.

JULIA. If you'd stop trying to get dramatic effects and tell me what it's all about—

JANE. (*Handing her a postcard.*) Read that.

JULIA. It's the Blue Grotto at Capri.

JANE. (*Impatiently.*) Yes, I know it is, but read it.

JULIA. (*Turning it over.*) Oh, my God! (*She reads it carefully.*)

JANE. There now!

JULIA. This is frightful. (*She rings bell.*)

JANE. What are you ringing for?

JULIA. I want a glass of water.

JANE. What are we going to do?

JULIA. Think—we must think! (*Enter* SAUNDERS.) Two glasses of water, please, Saunders.

SAUNDERS. Yes, ma'am. (*She goes out.*)

JULIA. When is he coming?

JANE. Now, I suppose—today—any moment!

JULIA. Oh, Jane, I wonder if he's changed?

JANE. No, I shouldn't think so—that type never does.

JULIA. Don't say "that type" like that—it's most irreverent.

(*Re-enter* SAUNDERS *with two glasses of water on a salver.*)

JANE. (*Taking one.*) Thank you very much.

JULIA. (*Also taking one.*) Thank you, Saunders.

(*Exit* SAUNDERS.)

JANE. I packed just a few things very hurriedly—I thought perhaps Brighton for a few days until our passports were properly viséd.

JULIA. Passports?

JANE. Yes, for America.

JULIA. Don't be ridiculous.

JANE. I'm sorry. I'm sorry. I'm all worked up—it was

a most frightful shock, and the funny thing is that I had
a presentiment when I woke this morning.

JULIA. So did I.

JANE. There, now!

JULIA. We must keep calm and talk it over quietly, it's
the only way. Have a cigarette. (*She hands* JANE *box.*)

JANE. (*Taking one.*) Oh, thank you.

JULIA. (*Also taking one and lighting both.*) Now then,
we've got the whole day before us.

JANE. (*Fervently.*) I only hope we have.

JULIA. You don't think he'll arrive before lunch?

JANE. He might. He might. He never had the slightest
restraint. Oh, after five years, I do think it's cruel! (*She
takes off her hat.*)

JULIA. It might have happened before; that would
have been much, much worse.

JANE. I don't know. I wonder. We might have had
more strength to resist.

JULIA. Oh no, dear, we've never been exactly bursting
with that kind of strength.

JANE. (*Intensely.*) You know what we are, don't you?
We're the slaves of coincidence, and we always have
been, it does make life so dreadfully difficult!

JULIA. Yes, but easier at moments; we can at least
face it together.

JANE. It's going to be agony—facing *him* together.

JULIA. We must be firm; after all, we're not in love
with him any more.

JANE. Not at the moment—but suppose when he
arrives he's just as attractive and glamorous as ever.
Oh, we shall both go down like ninepins.

JULIA. I shan't. I know, Jane, I shan't. I've changed
in seven years. I'm too fond of Fred.

JANE. Yes? I've been bolstering myself up like that all
the morning, arguing that I'm too fond of Willy. Everything's quite different now. . . . But I don't know—I'm
afraid—terribly afraid. You see, Julia, we have got to
face facts—we're not really *in love* with our husbands
any more. I had a scene with Willy about it only last

night. We're awfully happy, and there's a lovely firm basis of comradeship and affection and all that, but the real "being in love" part is dead! Well, you couldn't expect anything else after all this time.

JULIA. Yes, I told Fred all that this morning.

JANE. Oh, Julia, I do wish we hadn't—when we did!

JULIA. It's a fat lot of use wishing that now.

JANE. Hey, you, give me back the Blue Grotto.

JULIA. (*Handing it to her.*) It's typical of him to send that, anyhow. Typical.

JANE. (*Looking at it.*) Maurice! Maurice! It gives me a fearful sort of illegitimate thrill even to look at his name.

JULIA. (*Warningly.*) Now then, Jane!

JANE. I wonder if he realizes he's been the one grand passion in both our lives?

JULIA. Of course he does; it's almost his profession.

JANE. Our love for our husbands—that's been on an entirely different plane all along—nicer, worthier, and all that sort of thing, but not half so soul-shattering.

JULIA. I wonder if he can speak English now?

JANE. I hope not, he was so lovely in French.

JULIA. What would Willy and Fred say if they knew?

JANE. (*Shuddering.*) Oh, don't!

JULIA. Fred, I think, would be sensible, after the first shock had worn off.

JANE. Willy wouldn't.

JULIA. It isn't as if we'd been unfaithful *since* marriage—after all, it all happened before.

JANE. Yes, but men never forgive that sort of thing, no matter when it happened.

JULIA. It seems so unfair that men should have the monopoly of wild oats.

JANE. They haven't—but it's our duty to make them think they have.

JULIA. When I think of Italy, and the cypresses and the moonlight and the glorious romance of it all—

JANE. Don't, dear, you'll only upset yourself.

JULIA. Do you remember how I wrote to you in Scotland and told you all about it? (*Far away.*) Oh, how I adored him! And nobody knew—nobody knew a thing. I left Aunt Mary a week earlier than I said—and got out of the train at Pisa—he was waiting for me—we used to do and look at the Leaning Tower night after night—

JANE. Yes, and I was so worried because I guessed—

JULIA. And then that lovely song he used to sing all the time—sometimes on the terribly cracked piano at the hotel, and sometimes just walking along the street. (*Begins to sing.*) "Un peu d'amour . . ."

JANE. Julia, please, don't—don't! Because he used to sing that song to *me*, afterwards—

(JULIA *keeps singing, and* JANE *joins in. They are singing together when* SAUNDERS *crosses from the kitchen to answer the front door. She sings a couple of bars with them. They are rather annoyed.* SAUNDERS *enters with a postcard on a salver. She takes it to* JULIA.)

SAUNDERS. The post, madam.

JULIA. (*Jumps slightly—in stifled tones.*) That will do, Saunders.

(*Exit* SAUNDERS.)

JANE. (*With her eyes tight shut.*) Don't tell me, I know—it's the Leaning Tower of Pisa.

JULIA. Of course.

JANE. Oh, what a devil!

JULIA. (*Reading.*) "J'arriverai a Londres cette semaine —j'espere avec tout mon coeur que vous me n'oubliez pas. Maurice." Cette semaine!

JANE. And today's Saturday! What are we going to do?

JULIA. Listen, Jane, we're in for a bitter time. We must summon up all our courage and face it properly. Have another cigarette. (*Handing her box.*) We must get the whole situation laid out quite clearly, like Patience, then we shall know where we are. (*Sitting back on sofa.*) Now then—

JANE. Well, now then what?

JULIA. (*In businesslike tones.*) Two wretchedly happy married women—

JANE. Yes.

JULIA. Both during the first two years of their married lives having treated their exceedingly nice husbands to the requisite amount of passion and adoration—

JANE. Yes—yes!

JULIA. —after a certain time the first ecstasies of passion and adoration subside, leaving in some instances an arid waste of discontent—

JANE. Yes—lovely, darling. Yes?

JULIA. In some instances rank boredom and rampant adultery on both sides.

JANE. Don't be gross, Julia.

JULIA. And in other rare instances, such as ours—complete happiness and tranquillity devoid of violent emotions of any kind with the possible exception of golf.

JANE. Quite.

JULIA. Quite. And there lies the trouble—the lack of violent emotion, fireworks, etc.

JANE. I don't want fireworks.

JULIA. Neither do I—not the nice part of me, but there's a beastly, unworthy thing in both of us waiting to spring—it sprang before our marriage, and it's waiting to spring again—it hasn't been fed for a long time—

JANE. (*Shocked.*) Julia!

JULIA. To put it mildly, dear, we're both ripe for a lapse.

JANE. (*Going into peals of laughter.*) No, it's a relapse! Oh, dear!

JULIA. (*Also collapsing.*) It's perfectly appalling, and we're laughing on the very edge of an abyss!

JANE. I can't help it, it's sheer hysteria.

JULIA. We both happened to throw our respective bonnets over the same windmill—

JANE. (*Giggling weakly.*) Oh, do stop!

JULIA. (*Relentlessly.*) And in a critical moment in our matrimonial careers, that windmill is coming to wreck us.

JANE. (*Wailing.*) Yes, but I don't want to be wrecked! I don't want to be wrecked!

JULIA. Ssshh! Saunders will hear you.

JANE. (*Panic-stricken.*) Julia, don't you see? What I suggested in the first place, it's our only way—we must go—at once—anywhere out of London!

JULIA. I shall do no such thing—it would be most cowardly.

JANE. A blind goat could see through that, dear.

JULIA. All the same, I shall stay and face it.

JANE. If you do, I shall.

JULIA. There is not the least necessity for us both to suffer.

JANE. If you imagine I should enjoy being by myself in Brighton while you were gallivanting about London with Maurice, you're very much mistaken.

JULIA. I should be too much upset to gallivant.

JANE. No, dear, it won't do.

JULIA. What do you mean, "it won't do"?

JANE. We stand or fall together.

JULIA. I don't mind standing together, but I won't fall together—it would be most embarrassing.

JANE. Anyway, I am not going to be left out of anything.

JULIA. Very well then, I'll go away and you can stay.

JANE. (*Eagerly.*) Yes. Yes. That's all right!

JULIA. What about standing or falling together?

JANE. (*Nobly.*) Well, you see, I'm willing to sacrifice myself for *you*.

JULIA. Liar!

JANE. Julia, how can you?

JULIA. I thought so.

JANE. (*Airily.*) I don't know what you mean!

JULIA. Oh yes, you do.

JANE. If you're going to be cross, I shall go.

JULIA. I'm not in the least bit cross. I'm just seeing through you, that's all.

JANE. Seeing through me! But who was it who wouldn't leave London today because it would be cowardly? Huh!

JULIA. (*Sweetly.*) Are you insinuating, dear, that I *want* to stay?

JANE. Not insinuating, dear, I'm dead certain of it.

JULIA. (*Laughing forcedly.*) Ha, ha! Really, Jane!

JANE. You're simply longing for him.

JULIA. Jane!

JANE. You are, you know you are!

JULIA. So are you!

JANE. Certainly I am.

JULIA. Oh, Jane, we must be very careful.

JANE. I'm always careful.

JULIA. I don't mean about him, I mean about us.

JANE. Oh!

JULIA. Don't you see what's going to happen?

JANE. Yes—yes, I do!

JULIA. It's always the way, when sex comes up it wrecks everything. It's a beastly, rotten thing—

JANE. It didn't wreck us before.

JULIA. We weren't together before. If we had been, we should have been the blackest enemies in five minutes.

JANE. Yes—as it was you were a bit upset when I met him afterwards.

JULIA. I was awfully sweet about it.

JANE. It was too late for you to be anything else. I took jolly good care not to let you know until it was all over.

JULIA. Yes, that's true.

JANE. We've been friends, great friends, ever since we were eight and nine respectively—

JULIA. And in all probability this will break all that up.

JANE. Certainly—unless we are cunning.

JULIA. (*Firmly.*) Well, I won't go away.

JANE. Neither will I—we're both firmly agreed on *that* point.

JULIA. It's only natural, after all, that we should want to see him again.

JANE. And it's also only natural that when we do see him again, we shall fight like tigers.

JULIA. Oh, Jane darling, do you think we will really?

JANE. It's unavoidable. We almost started just now out of sheer anticipation.

JULIA. Oh, Jane darling, how miserable I am!

JANE. Nonsense, you're thoroughly thrilled and excited.

JULIA. Not altogether; I'm torn between my better self and my worse self. I never realized there were two of me until this moment so clearly defined. I want terribly badly to be a true, faithful wife, and look after Fred and live in peace, and I want terribly to have violent and illicit love made to me and be frenziedly happy and supremely miserable.

JANE. We're both in the same boat. But the most awful contingency is that one of us may give in utterly, leaving the other shrouded forever in unrewarded virtue.

JULIA. Meaning the one he fancies most?

JANE. Exactly.

JULIA. Well, there won't be any virtue at all—just biting jealousy.

JANE. We must make a vow that however badly one or both of us behaves during the black and scarlet period before us—when it's all over and died down, we can reinstate ourselves on the same concrete basis of friendship and intimacy without the slightest sacrificing of pride on either side.

JULIA. Oh yes, yes, Jane darling, I vow it now!

JANE. (*Kissing her.*) Darling! So do I—whatever we do—

JULIA. —and whatever we say—

JANE. —when temporarily unhinged by sex—

JULIA. —afterwards—perfect friendship—

JANE. —and *no* apologies!

JULIA. Not one. (*Suddenly*.) Jane, I can't go through with it after all.

JANE. Now, Julia—you made a vow—

JULIA. I'm sorry, I can't. It would be too frightful.

JANE. Agony.

JULIA. Let's do your plan, and fly.

JANE. Together?

JULIA. (*Impatiently*.) Yes, oh yes—together!

JANE. He'll think it so rude.

JULIA. Don't weaken, Jane.

JANE. Frenchmen are so particular about that sort of thing.

JULIA. It can't be helped, one can carry good manners too far.

JANE. We ought to be hospitable.

JULIA. Well, as neither of us can be hospitable without giving him the run of the house, we might as well leave him to freeze on the doorstep.

JANE. I know—we can leave him a letter.

JULIA. Of course, saying we've been called away.

JANE. Yes—that would ease my conscience.

JULIA. Now you write it while I pack a few things. Saunders! Saunders!

JANE. Your French is much better than mine.

JULIA. Never mind—I'll help. (*Enter* SAUNDERS.) Saunders, I want you to pack a small suitcase—I've been called away . . .

SAUNDERS. Yes, ma'am. (*They* BOTH *go off into bedroom, leaving door open*.)

JANE. (*On sofa*.) Shall I start "Mon cher Maurice"?

JULIA. (*Off*.) No, "Notre cher"—it's less compromising.

JANE. (*After writing for a moment*.) All right. Listen. "Notre cher Maurice, Nous sommes desolees, ce n'est pas possible pour nois de vous voir cette fois. . . ."

JULIA. (*Off*.) Not "cette fois," it sounds so sly.

JANE. What shall I put?

JULIA. While you are in London— No, Saunders, I shan't need these sort of things at all—

JANE. What's while?

JULIA. I haven't the faintest idea.

SAUNDERS. "Pendant," Madam.

JANE. Oh, you speak French, Saunders?

SAUNDERS. Yes, ma'am.

JULIA. Good gracious!

JANE. Good gracious nothing. It's wonderful. Saunders, how would you say, "We are very happily married?"

SAUNDERS. "Nous sommes mariees maintenant tres hereusement"—

JANE. Thank you. You really are a treasure, Saunders!

SAUNDERS. Thank you, ma'am.

JULIA. Do you think this is quite the moment to announce that we're happily married?

JANE. Now or never.

JULIA. Well, put "isn't it fun" after it.

JANE. I don't know how to.

JULIA. Saunders will.

SAUNDERS. "C'est amusant, n'est ce pas?"

JANE. C'est amusant, n'est-ce pas! Yes, but it isn't particularly. Besides he'll think it so facetious.

JULIA. It probably will be to him, he'll roar with laughter.

JANE. Oh, very well. (*She writes.*)

JULIA. Put "have you got a beard yet?"

JANE. (*Laughing, she writes.*) Oh! Wouldn't it be awful if he had!

JULIA. Yes, but much less dangerous.

JANE. Saunders, is beard masculine or feminine?

JULIA. Make it feminine, he'll appreciate it more. That's right, Saunders, in the top drawer, with my stockings.

JANE. (*Writing hard.*) I think that's all that's necessary now.

JULIA. Tidy up, Saunders. (*She enters in travelling things carrying a small suit case.*) Yes, dear, finish it off gracefully.

JANE. "Nous esperons pour vous voir quelquefois bientot." We must put that, it's mere politeness.

JULIA. Yes. Now we'll both sign our names. (*They sign their names. They then notice that they are both wearing hats trimmed with almost identical birds. With a little cry* JULIA *runs back into her room to change hers.*)

JANE. I'll get an envelope.

JULIA. (*Off.*) I think perhaps we ought to explain to Fred and Willy, don't you?

JANE. We haven't time to leave any more notes, we'll telephone.

JULIA. Where from?

JANE. Aberdeen! Come on!

JULIA. Saunders, we're leaving a note for a foreign gentleman when he calls. (*As she comes out of her bedroom having changed her hat.*)

SAUNDERS. (*Off.*) Very good, ma'am.

JANE. All right, I'm ready.

JULIA. I'm glad! I'm tremendously glad—we're doing the right thing—don't you feel marvellous?

JANE. No—awful!

JULIA. Never mind—our better selves have won, in spite of everything.

JANE. Yes.

(*They go towards the door with their bags. They almost reach it, when there comes a LOUD RING and KNOCK at the front door. They both stand still as though they had been struck—looking at one another. Then with one accord they plank down their bags.*)

JULIA. It's Maurice!

JANE. You're right.

JULIA. We're sunk.

JANE. I suppose so.

JULIA. (*With determination.*) Anyhow, it will be good for our French.

CURTAIN

ACT TWO

AT RISE: *When the CURTAIN rises* JULIA *is looking out of the window.* JANE *is seated on the chair Right of table. They are both elaborately dressed. The dinner table is laid for two and there are some lovely flowers in the room.*

JANE. I'm extremely hungry, Julia.

JULIA. So am I—ravenous.

JANE. It's getting on for nine.

JULIA. I know.

JANE. There's not the least likelihood of him arriving at this time.

JULIA. He might, especially if the Paris train were late.

JANE. We don't know whether he was coming from Paris.

JULIA. Where else could he be coming from?

JANE. Don't snap at me, Julia—he might be coming from the Channel Islands, or Brussels—he's frightfully cosmopolitan.

JULIA. I'm quite certain that he's coming from Paris.

JANE. Well, anyway, the idea was for him to arrive unexpectedly, discover us dining together in charming domestic surroundings, not sitting twiddling our thumbs with eager strained expressions, with the room decorated like a Bridal Suite.

JULIA. That, dear, was not in the best of taste. (SAUNDERS *enters.*) What have you got there, Saunders?

SAUNDERS. Salted almonds, madam.

JULIA. Oh, good.

JANE. Are you hungry, Saunders?

SAUNDERS. No, madam. I've already eaten.

JANE. Oh, you have.

JULIA. Will you have an almond?

25

JANE. Well—it may assuage the pangs a little.

JULIA. (*Takes plate to* JANE.) The table looks pretty, doesn't it?

JANE. (*Weakly.*) Lovely, darling.

JULIA. I'm sorry I haven't got a pebble for you to suck to take away your hunger. (SAUNDERS *giggles, back to audience at serving table.*) What are you smiling at, Saunders?

SAUNDERS. I'm so sorry, ma'am—

JULIA. You were going to say something?

SAUNDERS. If you'll allow me to, ma'am. Pebbles are not sucked to take away hunger, but thirst.

JULIA. Oh yes, I know that, all right.

SAUNDERS. In hot climates pebbles are sucked a great deal—they're sucked by the nomads in the desert.

JULIA. Oh, really now! I suppose you were in the desert yourself?

SAUNDERS. That's right. I was in the desert with the Red Cross. I also visited several desert stations when I was with Ensa. Pebbles are also wonderful for stammerers. Demosthenes said—

JULIA. Oh, yes, yes—very fine philosopher, wasn't he, a man with a great beard—

SAUNDERS. They are also very helpful with articulation, are a great help for elocution, and quite remarkable for developing the muscles of the tongue, and certainly—

JULIA. Thank you, Saunders. Curtain!

SAUNDERS. Very good, madam. (*Goes out.*)

JULIA. She makes me thirsty, with her talk of pebbles. It's been the most shattering day.

JANE. I shall never forget your face when, after all that suspense, the plumber arrived.

JULIA. I'm thankful he did, all the same.

JANE. Why?

JULIA. Domestic reasons.

JANE. And why do you suppose that Violet Coswick chose today of all days to come to tea?

JULIA. And talk exclusively of Paris and Frenchmen—

JANE. She has a very unpleasant mind, poor Violet, I suppose it must be the result of so much repression.

JULIA. Repression of what, dear?

JANE. Everything.

JULIA. She lacks opportunities—it's her clothes, I think.

JANE. They don't lack opportunities—they grab them wholeheartedly.

JULIA. I've never seen so many things on one woman.

JANE. And what was the meaning of that hat?

JULIA. It appeared to be kept on by suction. Shall we have a drink?

JANE. Oh no, not on empty tummies.

JULIA. (*Ringing bell.*) I shall get deep depression if we don't.

JANE. (*Resigned.*) We shall lapse into complete silliness and when Maurice does come we shall giggle helplessly at him and our heads will wobble.

JULIA. (*As* SAUNDERS *enters.*) Martinis, please, Saunders. Strong ones.

JANE. Oh, Julia!

JULIA. (*Firmly.*) Very strong ones.

SAUNDERS. Yes, ma'am.

JULIA. And if one isn't enough, we shall have two.

JANE. Not on your life!

SAUNDERS. If you will allow me to say so, ma'am, several drinks never do any harm. It is only the first which is dangerous, after that the damage is done.

JANE. Obviously you speak from experience.

SAUNDERS. I used to be a barmaid, madam. (*She goes out.*)

JULIA. Well, all I ask is that she was never an item in the News of the World!

JANE. (*Plaintively.*) Julia . . . Julia—I don't believe he ever will come.

JULIA. Neither do I. It's probably all an elfin joke—he was always being elfin.

JANE. And so terribly unreliable.

JULIA. I wouldn't trust him an inch.

JANE. *I* never did.

JULIA. All the same, he was a darling.

JANE. Adorable, damn him!

JULIA. And he doesn't know many people in England.

JANE. I think he *will* come.

JULIA. So do I.

JANE. And he'll kiss our hands and look up at us while he does it—you remember?

JULIA. I remember all right.

JANE. And then he'll laugh and show all his teeth.

JULIA. Many more than are usual.

JANE. I say, you know what we're doing, don't you?

JULIA. What?

JANE. Working ourselves up.

JULIA. We have been all day.

JANE. I should like to scream—scream and scream—and roll around on the floor—

JULIA. So should I—but we must restrain ourselves.

JANE. It's want of food.

JULIA. That's what it is.

(SAUNDERS *comes in with cocktails.*)

JANE. Oh, don't let's wait any longer.

JULIA. All right. (*She takes cocktail and takes glass to* JANE.) Dinner, please, Saunders.

JANE. And quickly.

SAUNDERS. Very good, ma'am. Shall I open the champagne?

JANE. (*Imploringly.*) Not yet.

JULIA. Yes, yes. Open it. Champagne is a great strengthener.

SAUNDERS. Very great, ma'am. The patients where I used to work—

JULIA. (*Exasperated.*) Oh, yes. Of course, she worked in a hospital.

SAUNDERS. How ever did you guess, ma'am?

JULIA. I think perhaps it's something about the way you walk.

SAUNDERS. My walk? I don't understand what you mean.

JULIA. No, neither do I, Saunders. You may serve dinner now.

SAUNDERS. Very good, madam. (*Goes out.*)

JULIA. If she goes on I shall throw her through the door.

JANE. Listen! There's a taxi, it's stopping outside.

JULIA. Quick! (*They* BOTH *rush to the window and peer out.*)

JANE. It's too dark—I can't see.

JULIA. He's got a black hat.

JANE. It must be—it must be.

JULIA. Oh no, it's the beastly woman from upstairs—how dare she drive about in taxis.

JANE. Oh, look, there's another coming round the corner. (*They* BOTH *crane to see.*)

SAUNDERS. (*Re-enters with oysters.*) Dinner is served, ma'am.

JANE. (*As they return to the table with great dignity.*) It was lovely of you to think of oysters, dear.

JULIA. They do give one a "grand" feeling. It's awfully necessary for us to feel "grand" tonight.

JANE. Wouldn't it be awful if Fred and Willy came home!

JULIA. (*With a warning look towards* SAUNDERS.) Shhh!

JANE. Drunk.

JULIA. What do you mean?

JANE. I said wouldn't it be dreadful if Fred and Willy came home drunk?

JULIA. Why should they?

JANE. (*Grimacing towards* SAUNDERS.) Don't be silly, Julia.

JULIA. Oh—yes, of course, frightful. I'd forgotten it was Saturday.

JANE. Saturday?

JULIA. Yes, naturally depressing in November because of the fog.

JANE. Yes, of course, but only if you pay your subscription in advance—

(SAUNDERS, *having served champagne and oysters, goes out.*)

JULIA. Poor Saunders.

JANE. She looked extremely startled.

JULIA. You really must be more careful, Jane.

JANE. I'm sorry, but I quite forgot she was there.

JULIA. I say, wouldn't it be too wonderful if he arrived suddenly now?

JANE. I should choke.

JULIA. You're sure you left a thoroughly clear message at your flat in case he went there first?

JANE. Of course.

JULIA. We're bound to get the most frightful shock when we do see him.

JANE. Well, I don't really see why.

JULIA. He's bound to have got fat, or something.

JANE. No, no, he won't have changed; he wouldn't come at all if he had because he's far too conceited.

JULIA. Oh no, not conceited, a little vain perhaps, naturally.

JANE. With those eyes who can blame him?

JULIA. And those hands—

JANE. And teeth—

JULIA. And legs! Oh, Jane!

JANE. Oh, Julia!

(*Re-enter* SAUNDERS *with* "Oeufs au plat Bercy" *on separate dishes.*)

JULIA. The cushions of the carriages are always so dusty, I find.

JANE. She ought never to have been burnt at the stake because she was such a very nice girl.

JULIA. I can hardly wait for strawberries to come in again.

SAUNDERS. (*Putting dish before* JANE.) Be careful, ma'am—it's very hot.

JANE. Thank you, I will.

JULIA. Will you have some more champagne?

JANE. No, thank you.

JULIA. Oh, come on, do—

JANE. Well, tidge it up! (*She holds out her glass, and* JULIA *fills it.*)

JULIA. (*Filling her own.*) I'm feeling much better, now, aren't you?

JANE. Yes, I adore this little sausage with my egg.

JULIA. It is sweet, isn't it?

(SAUNDERS *goes out.*)

JANE. (*Leaning back.*) It's all been such a wonderful adventure.

JULIA. It hasn't started yet.

JANE. Oh, yes, it has—I've enjoyed today enormously.

JULIA. Oh, Jane, how can you! It's been damnable!

JANE. Yes, but it's been so exciting. And I do love something to break the monotony.

JULIA. Don't be "young," Jane.

JANE. You're being very superior, but you're just as thrilled as I am.

JULIA. I see such blackness ahead if we're not careful.

JANE. We mustn't lose our heads.

JULIA. Perhaps he won't want us to this time.

JANE. Oh! (*She thinks about this, then after a look of disappointment goes back to her meal.*) I suddenly have beastly pangs about Fred and Willy.

JULIA. So have I.

JANE. We're being so disloyal.

JULIA. Yes, but only in thought so far.

(*The TELEPHONE rings.*)

BOTH. My God! I'll go.

JANE. (*Rising.*) I'll go.

JULIA. (*Also rising.*) It's my house.

JANE. Quick—toss for it—rough or smooth? (*She picks up a fork.*)

JULIA. Rough.

JANE. (*Tossing it.*) Rough it is.

JULIA. (*At telephone.*) Hallo! Yes, Park 8720—yes—Hallo—yes, speaking— (*She jumps.*) It is—it is—is that you, Maurice?

JANE. (*Rushing up and trying to hear.*) It can't be—it can't be—

JULIA. (*Crossly.*) Oh, Uncle Hugo, is that you—

JANE. Oh!

JULIA. I thought it was someone else.

JANE. Oh damn!

JULIA. He's playing golf with Willy—

JANE. Oh—damn—damn—damn—

JULIA. Shut up, Jane— What, Uncle Hugo? Yes, all right, I'll tell him—good-bye.

JANE. Stupid old fool.

JULIA. I hate all Fred's relations, anyway. (*They go back to the table.*)

JANE. He's probably gone straight to an hotel, will have a lovely hot bath, change his clothes, and come on here after.

JULIA. I wonder.

JANE. Oh yes. He always had a bath after a journey, remember.

JULIA. I hadn't forgotten, dear.

JANE. And he'll wear a soft silk shirt with his dinner-jacket—so beautifully careless.

JULIA. Do stop, Jane, you're making me feel dreadful.

JANE. (*Dreamily.*) I can see him now, threading his way between the tables outside Florian's on the Piazza San Marco—we used to have coffee there always, and then stroll languidly along the Piazetta—I wore a lovely green shawl—and then drift over the lagoon—hitch our gondola to a serenata and lie back and look up at the stars while darling little men in soft shirts poured out their sentimental souls in the most shattering tenor voices. Sometimes we wouldn't stop at all—

JULIA. No.

JANE. —but just glide on over the Picolo Canales until we suddenly came out into the big lagoon behind Venice —away from everywhere—just one or two buildings rising up like ghosts through the mist, then Maurice would take me in his arms and the world seemed to go . . .

(SAUNDERS *enters with Tournedos and sauce Bearnaise and Pommes Dauphine.*)

JULIA. The worst of a circus is, I'm always so *terrified* that they ill-treat the animals.

JANE. Poor George, oh poor George, and he *was* so charming before he married.

JULIA. I hope you haven't forgotten the sauce Bearnaise, Saunders?

SAUNDERS. No, ma'am—it's here.

JANE. I'm sure it'll be most delicious.

JULIA. Have some more champagne?

JANE. All right.

JULIA. (*Refilling both glasses.*) We ought to have some of those little wooden things in coloured paper to take the gassiness out.

JANE. They're such fun!

(*There is a sudden LOUD RING of the front door bell.* JULIA *gives a cry, and* JANE, *who is drinking, chokes.*)

JULIA. Pull yourself together, Jane.

JANE. (*Choking badly.*) I can't—it's agony—

JULIA. Leave the potatoes, and answer the door.

SAUNDERS. Very good, ma'am. Eat a little soft bread, ma'am.

JANE. (*Recovering a little.*) Oh, don't let him in—not yet—

JULIA. (*To* SAUNDERS.) Go on. (*To* JANE.) Eat some

bread—Saunders told you to—and she always knows best. (*She rushes round the table and administers bread and water to* JANE.)

JANE. It's all right now. I'm better. (*She rises and grabs her bags, then proceeds to powder her nose frantically.*)

SAUNDERS. (*Re-enters.*) It's a foreign gentleman, ma'am.

JULIA. Why didn't you show him in?

SAUNDERS. He says he won't come in. He only wants to know if there's a Madame Gambelitti living here.

JANE. What's he like?

SAUNDERS. Quite respectable, ma'am, but with a long moustache.

JULIA. Come on, Jane, we'll peep. (*They go to the door and peer round into the hall—and then return to the table crestfallen.*) Why didn't you tell him there was no Madame Whatshername here, and get rid of him?

SAUNDERS. You said you were expecting a foreign gentleman, ma'am, and I thought I'd better keep him in case.

JULIA. Well, get rid of him now.

SAUNDERS. Very good, ma'am. (*Exits.*)

JANE. (*Almost in tears.*) It's downright cruel, that's what it is.

JULIA. It's the first time that anybody not aggressively English has rung that bell since we came here.

JANE. And he would come after his beastly Madame Gambelitti tonight of all nights. It's indecent!

JULIA. More champagne?

JANE. (*Loudly.*) No, thank you.

JULIA. Well, don't shout.

JANE. I shall shout if I like, Julia; you mustn't be dictatorial.

JULIA. (*Fills both glasses again.*) Let's have a toast!

JANE. (*Rising and holding up her glass.*) Maurice Duclos.

JULIA. (*Also rising.*) Maurice Duclos! No heel taps. (BOTH *drain their glasses.*)

JANE. (*Sitting down quickly.*) That was silly of us.

JULIA. (*Also sitting.*) No heel taps. Eat some steak quickly. (*There is silence for a moment while they devote themselves to their food.*)

JANE. Julia, wouldn't it be awful if a tree blew down and killed Fred and Willy on the golf links?

JULIA. (*Shocked.*) Jane, how can you?

JANE. It would serve us right.

JULIA. It would be too awful—I should never forgive myself.

JANE. Neither should I.

JULIA. There's a frightful gale blowing.

JANE. Oh, the wind. Such things do happen.

JULIA. No, they don't—not if you don't think about them. It's mind over matter.

JANE. Julia, I do admire you, because you're so strong and sensible.

JULIA. Nonsense, dear, it's just that I'm not afraid of life.

JANE. You're brave.

JULIA. But I'm no braver than you, Jane darling.

JANE. We must both be brave always.

JULIA. (*Slightly maudlin.*) We must be brave always, whatever happens.

JANE. Even if Fred and Willy *were* killed we should have to bear it.

JULIA. Yes, Jane—we wouldn't break down, would we—we'd face the world with a smile.

JANE. Well, not quite a smile, because we might be misunderstood.

JULIA. Poor darling Fred, I can see Fred now being carried in on a stretcher—

JANE. There's Willy on another stretcher. Oh, dear— (*She breaks down.*)

JULIA. Jane, dear—don't—

(*Re-enter* SAUNDERS *with sweet—"Profiteroles au chocolat."*)

JANE. I don't want any more, because I've had enough.

JULIA. So have I, but we must go on, it will keep up our strength.

JANE. They look lovely. Tinker, tailor, soldier, sailor—

JULIA. (*Giggling.*) No, you do that with cherry stones.

JANE. (*Also giggling.*) I like doing it with these.

JULIA. Have some more champagne.

JANE. No, thank you.

JULIA. Here you are. (*She pours it out.*)

JANE. Thanks, darling.

JULIA. The silly part is that I'm now beginning to feel sleepy.

JANE. I'm not—I'm just cosy.

JULIA. No, I'm terribly, terribly sleepy. Bring in the coffee, Saunders.

(*Exit* SAUNDERS.)

JANE. Julia, what a pretty girl Saunders is.

JULIA. Yes, isn't she? A pretty girl . . .

JANE. Do you know, she ought to be a great success in life, because she's so calm.

JULIA. (*Suddenly bursting out laughing.*) Oh, dear—

JANE. What are you laughing at?

JULIA. You look frightfully funny.

JANE. What's the matter with me? (*She gets up just a little unsteadily and looks at herself in the glass.*)

JULIA. (*Giggling hopelessly.*) I don't know—you just do.

JANE. So do you. Go and look at yourself.

JULIA. (*Also getting up, and looking in the glass.*) It's our heads, I think. They're far too big.

JANE. That's 'cos we've had too much champagne.

JULIA. (*Agreeably.*) Much too much.

JANE. Let's sit down.

JULIA. All right. (*They return to the table.*)

JANE. I'm sorry I didn't know you'd booked permanently. Wouldn't it be awful if the Queen suddenly came in?

JULIA. I don't think she will—she's in Paris.

JANE. She's back.

JULIA. Anyway, Saunders would announce her.

JANE. I'm beginning to feel warm and comfortable.

JULIA. Yes, I'm feeling absolutely splendid myself. I couldn't feel better. A child could play with me.

(*The TELEPHONE rings.*)

JANE. The bell, the bell!

JULIA. It must be him this time.

JANE. It's my turn—come and stand close to me.

JULIA. All right—I'll sit on the edge of the sofa.

JANE. (*At telephone—loudly.*) Hallo!

JULIA. He is not deaf.

JANE. Hallo! Yes, this is Park 8724.

JULIA. No, it isn't.

JANE. Keep quiet, I can't hear.

JULIA. Do look on the thing. It isn't Park 8724.

JANE. (*Gives a quick look at telephone numbers.*) No, it isn't—it isn't—it's 8720—they've cut off. Julia, it's a trunk call; what *am* I to do? Exchange, hallo—

JULIA. Go on. Put back the receiver.

JANE. It will only go on ringing and ringing and ringing if I do. Exchange, hello— (*She bangs receiver up and down.*)

JULIA. Oh, come on, give it to me, for heaven's sake. (*She snatches the telephone out of* JANE's *hand.*) Hallo, this is a wrong number. No, I'm not; I'm somebody quite different. Oh, do shut up then. (*She slams receiver down.*) It's a shame! What on earth did you say we were Park 8724 for? You ought to know the number by now.

JANE. I couldn't help it, dear, because he jumped at me.

JULIA. Don't pull me like that. You were in such a flutter because you thought it was Maurice—

JANE. (*With dignity.*) I was as calm as a cucumber. I wish you wouldn't follow me around.

JULIA. Why you said it was Park 8724 I can't imagine.

JANE. I told you I couldn't help it.

JULIA. Don't argue, Jane, when one's been stupid over anything it's much better not to argue.

JANE. (*Irately.*) Stupid, indeed! I like that! Why, if you— (*The TELEPHONE rings.*) Oh, it's ringing. Isn't it pretty!

JULIA. Leave it to me.

JANE. It must be him.

JULIA. No, it's only that trunk call again. It'll probably go on all night because you told him it was Park 8720.

JANE. I didn't—I said Park 8724.

JULIA. Jane, how can you? You said 8720.

JANE. It *is* 8720.

JULIA. It isn't.

JANE. Look there. (*She shows her.*)

JULIA. I shall go mad, that's all, and it will serve you right. (*The TELEPHONE continues to ring.*)

JANE. Oh, stop it ringing. Stop it ringing!

JULIA. Very well—will that suit you? (*She takes off receiver and puts it behind her back over shoulder as* SAUNDERS *enters with coffee.*)

JANE. I don't mind what happens now—I'm just past everything.

JULIA. Will you have some coffee?

JANE. (*Taking it from* SAUNDERS.) Thank you.

JULIA. A liqueur?

JANE. (*Giggling.*) Don't be ridiculous.

JULIA. Benedictine, please, Saunders.

JANE. Shall we have them in tumblers?

JULIA. I ordered these Benedictines for you, I thought they would round off the meal so nicely.

JANE. They certainly will. (JULIA *hiccoughs.*) Pardon!

(SAUNDERS *goes to sideboard, pours out two liqueurs and puts them down on table, then goes out with the remains of the sweet on a tray.*)

JANE. (*Sipping her liqueur.*) It's terribly strong.

JULIA. (*Airily.*) Well, it's supposed to make you feel rather—rather— (*She waves her hand vaguely.*)

JANE. How thoughtful of you, dear.

JULIA. Will you have some fruit?

JANE. I couldn't.

JULIA. Do—it rounds off the meal so nicely.

JANE. For heaven's sake stop rounding off the meal, because it's getting on my nerves.

JULIA. Don't be so temperamental, Jane.

JANE. It's only a suggestion—do you think it would matter if I took off my shoes?

JULIA. Not in the least—they always do in Japan, I believe—quite an old custom.

JANE. (*Kicking off her shoes.*) If Maurice had any instincts he'd arrive now—looking marvelous.

JULIA. And make the most lovely sort of baffled scene.

JANE. What would baffle him?

JULIA. Us, of course, because we'd be so gloriously aloof and stately.

JANE. I shouldn't be aloof—I should give in without a murmur.

JULIA. Then he'd want me more.

JANE. If you think that's the way to make him, you'd better encourage me.

JULIA. You don't need any encouraging.

JANE. What do you mean by that?

JULIA. What I say.

JANE. Oh, yes of course.

JULIA. Anyway, Jane, I should never allow you to cheapen yourself.

JANE. (*Affronted.*) How dare you!

JULIA. How dare I what?

JANE. Insult me.

JULIA. I didn't insult you.

JANE. You did—you went too far—what you said was beyond a joke.

JULIA. It wasn't meant to be a joke—I hate jokes, bitterly.

JANE. Then you meant what I said?

JULIA. Meant what?

JANE. How can anyone carry on a conversation with you when you keep on saying what, what, what, what, what, what, what all the time? If you can't say what I grasp, you'd better go to bed.

JULIA. That was exceedingly rude of you, Jane.

JANE. I'm sorry, Julia, but you're annoying me.

JULIA. Unfortunately, this happens to be my flat.

JANE. (*Looking round.*) Never mind, you'll get used to it in time.

JULIA. Stop bickering, Jane.

JANE. How can I stop bickering when you sit there abusing me?

JULIA. I never abused you.

JANE. Yes, you did—you insinuated that I was brazen.

JULIA. Well, so you are brazen, sometimes—we all are, it's human nature to be brazen sometimes.

JANE. Nothing of the sort.

JULIA. Do stop contradicting everything I say—it's infuriating me now.

JANE. Who was it who wouldn't leave London this morning?

JULIA. Why should I want to leave London this morning? I'm very, very disappointed in you—I thought you had a nicer mind than that.

JANE. I suppose you think your mind is a lovely gilt basket filled with mixed fruit with a bow on the top?

JULIA. Better than being an old sardine tin with a few fins left in it.

JANE. You'll regret that remark in your soberer moments.

JULIA. Have a cigarette.

JANE. Thank you.

JULIA. A light?

JANE. (*With dignity.*) No, thank you.

JULIA. (*Grandly.*) Perhaps you'd like a little soft music?

JANE. Yes, if it would put you in a better temper.

JULIA. (*Ignoring her—conversationally.*) I had such an amusing letter from Aunt Harriet this morning.

JANE. (*Rudely.*) Did you, did you? I thought she was dead.

JULIA. (*With a superior frown.*) I think you must be muddling her up with someone else.

JANE. Go on, dear—tell me some more news. I love you when you're offended.

JULIA. (*Sadly.*) I'm not offended, Jane. A little hurt, perhaps, and surprised—

JANE. (*Suddenly furious.*) How dare you draw yourself up and become the outraged hostess with *me?*

JULIA. I'm sorry—I must have lost my sense of humour—perhaps because I'm tired—we've been together so much lately, I think we're grating on one another's nerves.

JANE. You're right. Now tell me, where are my shoes?

JULIA. (*Disdainfully.*) I really don't know—they can't have gone far.

JANE. I should like to shake you, shake you and shake you and shake you until your eyes drop out.

JULIA. Indeed?

JANE. Yes, when you're superior and grand like that you rouse the very worst in me—

JULIA. Obviously.

JANE. You make me feel like a French Revolution virago. Julia, I'd like to rush up and down Bond Street with one of your tiny heads on a pole.

JULIA. I think it would be as well for you to pull yourself together and I'll ask Saunders to help you to your flat.

JANE. If she comes near me I shall throttle her.

JULIA. I've never actually seen you violent before—it's very interesting psychologically.

JANE. (*With sudden determination.*) I could bring you down to earth in one moment if I liked.

JULIA. What vulgarity!

JANE. This is not vulgarity—it's something I was

more ashamed of than vulgarity, but I'm not ashamed of it any more, Julia. I've kept something from you.

JULIA. I wish you'd go home, Jane.

JANE. I must have realized all along you were going to turn out false and beastly—

JULIA. What are you talking about?

JANE. Never you mind what I'm talking about. Where are my shoes?

JULIA. Never mind about your shoes—what do you mean?

JANE. Give me my shoes.

JULIA. They're probably under the table—you'd better get them and go.

JANE. (*Finding them and putting them on savagely.*) And now I'm glad that I *did* keep it to myself.

JULIA. That's better.

JANE. I suppose you're still far too grand to be curious. It concerns Maurice.

JULIA. Oh, it concerns Maurice, does it?

JANE. Yes, I thought that would rouse you.

JULIA. I think you'd better tell me—if you don't want to wreck our friendship for ever.

JANE. It will certainly wreck our friendship when I *do* tell you—and I don't care. Julia—*I know where he is.*

JULIA. It's a lie.

JANE. No, it's true. He telephoned me while I was dressing tonight.

JULIA. Jane!

JANE. Yes, I didn't want to tell you because I thought it would have hurt your feelings. But now I know that you haven't got any feelings to hurt—only a shallow sort of social vanity—

JULIA. Where is he, then? Tell me.

JANE. I shall do nothing of the sort. I don't want you to rush round there and make a fool of yourself.

JULIA. (*Losing all control.*) How dare you! How dare you! I'll never speak to you again in all my life. You're utterly completely contemptible. If it's true, you're nothing but a snivelling hypocrite! If it's false, you're a bare-faced liar! There's nothing to choose between you! Please go at once!

JANE. Go—I'm only too delighted. You must curb your social sense, Julia, if it leads you to drunken orgies and abuse.

JULIA. (*In tears.*) Go—go—go away—

JANE. Certainly I shall—and it may interest you to know that I'm going *straight* to Maurice!

JULIA. (*Wailing.*) Liar—liar!

JANE. It's true. And I shall go away with him at once, and you and Fred and Willy can go to hell, the whole lot of you! (*Flounces out.*)

(JULIA *hurls herself on to the sofa in screaming hysterics.*)

CURTAIN

ACT THREE

SCENE: *The same. It is the next morning.*

AT RISE: JULIA *is finishing her breakfast gloomily. She rings the bell at her side.* SAUNDERS *comes in.*

SAUNDERS. Yes, Madam?

JULIA. When I say a "soft-boiled" egg, Saunders, I don't mean an *un*-boiled egg.

SAUNDERS. So long as I know, ma'am.

JULIA. There was also a long blonde hair in the marmalade.

SAUNDERS. (*Anxiously.*) Was there, ma'am?

JULIA. I haven't the remotest idea how it got there as we are both distinct brunettes; perhaps it was Mr. Smucker's.

SAUNDERS. Yes, ma'am.

JULIA. Anyway, please in future search the marmalade.

SAUNDERS. Very good, ma'am.

JULIA. I'm inclined against the theory that it was Mr. Smucker's, as there was also a hair in the milk you've just brought in.

SAUNDERS. Good gracious!

JULIA. See for yourself.

SAUNDERS. (*Looking.*) My!

JULIA. Perhaps it came from the milkman?

SAUNDERS. I don't think so.

JULIA. Why not?

SAUNDERS. The milkman is bald.

JULIA. That's sanitary.

SAUNDERS. It's a mystery, ma'am.

JULIA. It's no mystery, it's milk I cannot drink.

SAUNDERS. Very good, ma'am.

JULIA. You may clear away now.

SAUNDERS. Very good, ma'am. (JULIA *leaves the breakfast table and crosses to below sofa for cigarettes. Goes*

44

above sofa to telephone. Her head gives her rather a
sharp reminder of the previous evening's excesses. SAUN-
DERS *notices this and hastens to the kitchen to make up*
one of her remedies.) I think I have just the right thing
for your hang-over, madam.

JULIA. What's that? (SAUNDERS *has disappeared.*
JULIA *goes to the telephone and dials a number. Putting*
down the receiver.) Engaged! (*Looks out of window.*
SAUNDERS *comes back with glasses and spoon, one con-*
taining water and the other salts. She mixes the two by
pouring the water from one glass to the other.) What
have you got there?

SAUNDERS. I think you'll find this an excellent remedy.

JULIA. Oh no, I couldn't possibly!

SAUNDERS. Oh yes, try a little, ma'am. I once cured
twenty natives in an African—

JULIA, Oh, all right—all right—

SAUNDERS. How do you feel, madame?

JULIA. (*Drinks some of the salts while* SAUNDERS *clears*
away the breakfast things, then goes to the telephone
again.) Park 5703, yes 03. (*Quite suddenly she belches.*)
I'm sorry I've been troubled. I say, Saunders, it's doing
me good already.

SAUNDERS. I thought it would. The natives—

JULIA. (*Heading her off.*) I think you'd better stand
by with another in case I can get through to Mrs. Banbury.

SAUNDERS. Very good, ma'am. (*Exits.*)

JULIA. (*At the telephone.*) It can't possibly still be
engaged. My good woman, you suffer from both incom-
petence and stupidity. (*She replaces the receiver and*
picks up the newspaper. Reading.) Muriel Fenchurch!
I'm sick of Muriel Fenchurch!

(*There has been a ring at the front door and* SAUNDERS
has gone to answer it. WILLY *enters.* SAUNDERS *re-*
turns to the kitchen, giving WILLY *rather a pene-*
trating glance as she does so.)

WILLY. Good morning, Julia.

JULIA. Willy! What on earth are you doing here? Where's Fred?

WILLY. (*Gloomily.*) I left him at the Grand Hotel, Chichester.

JULIA. Where's Jane?

WILLY. Don't you know?

JULIA. I haven't the faintest idea—she might be anywhere by now.

WILLY. What do you mean "by now?"

JULIA. Just "by now."

WILLY. What's the matter?

JULIA. Nothing.

WILLY. What's happened?

JULIA. Oh, everything, probably—by now.

WILLY. What are you talking about?

JULIA. Oh, don't be tiresome, Willy!

WILLY. I made sure Jane would be with you. Where's she gone?

JULIA. Stop cross-questioning me—anyone would think I'd murdered her and put her in a box or something.

WILLY. Well, from the furtive way you're behaving I shouldn't be in the least surprised.

JULIA. Well, what about you? What do you mean by leaving Fred alone at the Grand Hotel, Chichester?

WILLY. We had a row last night.

JULIA. Oh, did you!

WILLY. Yes, Fred infuriated me.

JULIA. (*With sarcasm.*) I'm very sorry—I'll speak to him severely.

WILLY. Thank you! And I felt I couldn't bear to meet him at breakfast and go all over it again—so I crept out and left by the early train.

JULIA. What did you row about?

WILLY. Nothing.

JULIA. That's the worst kind.

WILLY. Have you quarrelled with Jane?

JULIA. Yes, bitterly.

WILLY. What about?

JULIA. Nothing.

WILLY. Oh!

JULIA. We got drunk.

WILLY. What!

JULIA. Extremely drunk.

WILLY. Julia!

JULIA. Well, Jane was much worse than I was—and, we quarrelled.

WILLY. (*Incensed.*) If I can't go away for a quiet game of golf without you making Jane drunk—

JULIA. I didn't make her—it was voluntary.

WILLY. Disgusting, I call it.

JULIA. She banged out of the flat.

WILLY. Where is she now?

JULIA. I don't know, and I don't care.

WILLY. Don't be callous, Julia.

JULIA. Probably at home in bed sleeping it off.

WILLY. She isn't—I've just been there.

JULIA. I thought you came straight here.

WILLY. No, I had a large bag and golf clubs.

JULIA. Are you sure that Jane isn't at home?

WILLY. Perfectly, but I didn't worry because I thought she'd be with you.

JULIA. (*Turning away.*) Then it *was* true, then—

WILLY. What was true?

JULIA. (*Biting her lip—angrily.*) Oh!—Oh!

WILLY. What's in God's name's the matter?

JULIA. I was going to ring her up and try to make friends again. I didn't believe for a moment—I never thought— Oh!

WILLY. Didn't believe what?

JULIA. She must have been steadily deceiving me all through dinner. How dare she! Oh, oh, oh! (*Begins striding up and down the room.*)

WILLY. Julia, will you stop still and explain what's happened?

JULIA. (*Stopping.*) I'll stop still and explain! Oh yes, I'll explain all right—the sly, underhand little—

WILLY. (*With dignity.*) Will you please remember that you are referring to my wife.

JULIA. Your wife—huh! Optimist!

WILLY. Julia!

JULIA. (*Irately.*) Oh Willy—my poor, poor Willy.

WILLY. You're maddening me, Julia.

JULIA. To think that she could behave like that—after all these years. Oh, it's contemptible!

WILLY. (*Catching her by the shoulder.*) What's happened to Jane? Where's she gone?

JULIA. I should like to break it to you gently, Willy—she's gone off with a man!

WILLY. What!

JULIA. (*Defiantly.*) A Frenchman.

WILLY. Nonsense, she can't have.

JULIA. I tell you she has.

WILLY. I don't believe it—you're unhinged.

JULIA. I'm perfectly hinged. It's true.

WILLY. I'm sorry, Julia, but I don't believe it. I know Jane too well; she'd never rush off like that at a moment's notice.

JULIA. (*Bitterly.*) She knew where he was all the time, and she went to him.

WILLY. She was pulling your leg.

JULIA. Don't be so pig-headed, Willy, this is one of the few big moments in your life, and you're behaving like a ninny.

WILLY. If you think stamping up and down the room and blackguarding Jane is a big moment in my life you're very much mistaken.

JULIA. (*Exasperated.*) But it's true! She's known him for years. She was in love with him before she married you—before she met you.

WILLY. Don't be ridiculous.

JULIA. Your smug complacency is beyond belief. I suppose you think that no woman would ever dare to leave you?

WILLY. Jane couldn't—she'd hate it.

JULIA. You're going to have a shattering awakening.

WILLY. I say, Julia, don't go on ramping any more—just calm down and explain things quietly. I'll pour myself out some coffee, if I may. (*He does so.*)

JULIA. (*Watches him in silence.*) Willy—I—oh! (*She bursts into tears.*)

WILLY. What's up now?

JULIA. I'm a beast—a traitress— (*She sobs.*)

WILLY. No, you're not—you're just thoroughly hysterical—you'll be better in a moment. (*He drinks some coffee.*)

JULIA. (*Controlling herself.*) But Willy—I'm sorry—but what I told you just now was true, Willy.

WILLY. (*Amiably.*) I'm trying hard to understand. I can't help feeling that there's something awfully silly behind all this—it doesn't seem to ring true.

JULIA. (*With sarcasm.*) I suppose you think I'm playing an amusing practical joke on you?

WILLY. No, it isn't that, but you've either deceived yourself into believing it or else you're making a mistake.

JULIA. But, Willy—

WILLY. If Jane really had left me, I know I should have some sort of feeling about it—but I haven't.

JULIA. Well, that'll come later.

WILLY. Who is this man she's supposed to be with?

JULIA. He's a Frenchman—Maurice Duclos. We both knew him before we married.

WILLY. Did you know him well?

JULIA. Extremely well.

WILLY. And Jane? Was Jane in love with him then?

JULIA. Yes, violently—we both were.

WILLY. Did you—er—did you—?

JULIA. Yes, Willy.

WILLY. Where?

JULIA. Pisa.

WILLY. And did Jane ever—?

JULIA. Yes, Willy.

WILLY. Good God, where?

JULIA. Venice, I think.

WILLY. This is horrible—incredible—

JULIA. Willy, I'm sorry I—

WILLY. (*Abruptly.*) You'd better save your apologies for Fred. I'm going to find Jane.

JULIA. Well, then, I'm coming with you, Willy.

WILLY. Has she seen this man since we've been married?

JULIA. No—at least—I don't know—she's such a liar.

WILLY. When did *you* last see him?

JULIA. Seven years ago on the railway station at Pisa. We were both going to Paris together, and at the last moment I wanted a salami sandwich, and as he hated garlic we had a row. He was far too temperamental, anyway, so I pushed him out on to the platform just as the train was starting. I regretted it bitterly at the time—but now I'm glad, I'm glad I did.

WILLY. I think you ought to be ashamed of yourself.

JULIA. I didn't push him very hard.

WILLY. I don't mean about that—I mean the whole affair.

JULIA. Willy, are you daring to disapprove of me?

WILLY. Yes, you're devoid of the slightest moral sense.

JULIA. What about Jane?

WILLY. Jane's different—she's just weak. You probably set her a bad example.

JULIA. I set her a bad example!

WILLY. (*Hotly.*) I wouldn't mind betting you met the beastly man first and then told Jane all about it and generally egged her on.

JULIA. She didn't need any egging—she met him and then she didn't tell anything about it for ages afterwards.

WILLY. She was probably too ashamed and repentant.

JULIA. Repentant my foot!

WILLY. Anyhow, it's more than you are—you're positively glorying in your—your—shame!

JULIA. If I'd known what a smug little man you were I'd never have let Jane marry you anyway.

WILLY. And if I'd known how utterly lacking you were in all the finer feelings I'd never have let Fred come near you.

JULIA. I should think it would be as well to stop hurl-
ing abuse at me and go in search of your weak but
strictly virtuous wife, who, if she hasn't succeeded in
finding Maurice Duclos by now, is probably roaming
about the streets in deep evening dress and hiccuping.

WILLY. You must come with me.

JULIA. No, I shall do no such thing.

WILLY. You said you would.

JULIA. That was before your insults to me.

WILLY. Julia, do come. Take off your apron.

JULIA. This dress has an apron.

WILLY. Oh, I beg your pardon. But please come.

JULIA. Where shall we go first, Bow Street?

WILLY. She can't have gone far.

JULIA. Judging by her condition when she left this flat
last night she might have gone further than our wildest
dreams.

WILLY. Please come, Julia.

JULIA. I'll come back to your flat—she may have left
a note or something.

WILLY. I never thought of that.

JULIA. Wait a moment. (*She goes into the bedroom
and issues forth in a small hat and a coat over her arm.*)

WILLY. Look here, Julia, I'm sorry for what I said just
now.

JULIA. And so you ought to be.

WILLY. But I still don't believe it all—quite.

JULIA. I want to make one thing perfectly clear to
you. I'm not coming with you because I wish to help you.
I'm coming because I wish to find Jane and tell her
exactly what I think of her.

WILLY. I say, Julia, don't be beastly to her. She's
probably feeling pretty awful.

JULIA. I don't care if she's feeling heavenly, she won't
be when I've finished with her. (*They go out.*)

(SAUNDERS *just catches sight of them as they vanish.*
SAUNDERS *gets a duster and a feather flick from a
drawer and begins to dust. She stops dusting when*

she reaches the piano and begins to play and hum. The TELEPHONE rings.)

SAUNDERS. (*At the telephone.*) Hallo! Is that Park 8720?—Yes—Mr. Sterroll's residence. Yes—Is Mrs. Sterroll in—no— When will she be back? I don't know, sir, she didn't say, yes, sir—what name, sir? One moment, sir—I'll write it down— (*She writes on the block.*) Maurice Duclos—Park 9264— Bien, Monsieur. Je n'y manquerai pas. Au revoir, Monsieur. (*Hangs up and returns to the piano.*)

FRED. (*Enters. Watches her for a while.*) Saunders!

SAUNDERS. (*Surprised.*) Oh, sir! You did give me a start.

FRED. What on earth are you doing?

SAUNDERS. Practising the piano, sir.

FRED. I think perhaps it would be better if you practised in the kitchen.

SAUNDERS. Yes, sir.

FRED. Where's the mistress?

SAUNDERS. She's gone out, sir.

FRED. Gone out? But it's pouring.

SAUNDERS. Yes, sir.

FRED. Where's she gone?

SAUNDERS. I don't know, sir.

FRED. She's upstairs with Mrs. Banbury, I expect. Run up, will you, and tell her I've come back?

SAUNDERS. Very good, sir, what number is it, sir?

FRED. Number five—two floors up.

SAUNDERS. Very good, sir. (*Goes out.*)

(FRED *lights a cigarette and wanders about the room aimlessly. He goes over to the piano and plays absently the tune of "Meme les Anges" with one finger. He also hums a little.*)

JANE. (*Enters rather draggled, in evening dress and a cloak.*) Fred! What are you doing?

FRED. (*Turning.*) Playing the piano. Good heavens!

JANE. What?

FRED. Have you been out all night?

JANE. Yes.

FRED. Lucky for you I left Willy at Chichester.

JANE. Oh, you did, did you?

FRED. Yes, sleeping like a hog. I left early in the car.

JANE. Why?

FRED. Well, as a matter of fact, we had rather a row last night. If you'll forgive me saying so, your husband is a fool sometimes.

JANE. I've always found him extremely intelligent.

FRED. Where have you been?

JANE. Mind your own business.

FRED. Don't jump down my throat—it was quite a harmless question.

JANE. I object to your dictatorial tone.

FRED. Well, to come in like that at eleven o'clock in the morning is a little—

JANE. If I choose to come in naked on a tricycle, it's no affair of yours. Where's Julia?

FRED. I don't know, she went out before I arrived.

JANE. Out—out where?

FRED. I haven't the faintest idea. I thought she'd probably be with you.

SAUNDERS. (*Re-enters.*) The mistress isn't at Mrs. Banbury's, sir. (*She sees* JANE.) Oh!

JANE. Don't look so startled, Saunders. You left the door open so I walked in.

SAUNDERS. Yes, ma'am.

FRED. Saunders, what time did the mistress go out?

SAUNDERS. Just before you came in, sir.

FRED. Was she alone?

SAUNDERS. No, sir, there was a gentleman with her.

JANE. (*Tensely.*) A what?

SAUNDERS. A gentleman, ma'am.

FRED. Who was it?

SAUNDERS. I don't know, sir, he didn't leave any name; he just walked straight in.

JANE. What was he like?

SAUNDERS. About medium height, ma'am, and dark.

JANE. (*Ominously.*) Dark, was he!

FRED. Why, what's the matter?

JANE. I'm extremely sorry for you, Fred, extremely sorry for you.

FRED. (*Startled.*) That will do, Saunders.

SAUNDERS. Very good, sir. (*She goes out.*)

FRED. Now then, Jane, what do you mean?

JANE. Don't speak to me for a moment, just don't speak to me— I'm trying to control myself.

FRED. (*Very puzzled.*) What's all this mystery about?

JANE. (*Austerely.*) There is no mystery, I'm afraid, any more—it's all far too clear.

FRED. Jane—tell me at once—what's happened?

JANE. Fred, you'll know all too soon enough. Julia *was* my friend—I have no intention of being disloyal.

FRED. Jane—tell me what's happened!

JANE. (*Sadly.*) I can't possibly. Julia may be double-faced, treacherous and thoroughly immoral. But I repeat, she *was* my friend.

FRED. (*Relieved.*) Oh, I see—you had a row last night, too.

JANE. Yes, we did.

FRED. What about?

JANE. I don't know—Julia spoke rather indistinctly.

FRED. Do you know where she's gone now?

JANE. I have a shrewd suspicion, but my lips are sealed.

FRED. Tell me at once.

JANE. I can't possibly. I— (*She catches sight of* MAURICE'S *name on the telephone block. She gives a gasp of fury.*) Oh no! Oh no!

FRED. What's the matter now?

JANE. So she knew—all the time—oh!

FRED. (*Frantically.*) Knew *what*?

JANE. How dare she—how dare she—it's contemptible—it's—oh— (*She takes up the telephone book and hurls it to the ground.*) The sneaking hypocrite. Oh, the despicable squalor of it all—to be deceived like that by

one's best friend, and for such a sordid purpose— Oh!
Oh!—Oh! (*She positively stamps with rage.*)

FRED. (*Picks up the block and reads name on it.*)
Who's this?

JANE. Don't speak to me—don't speak to me!

FRED. What does this mean?

JANE. It means that Julia has deserted you.

FRED. Deserted me?

JANE. Yes, she's gone off with that Frenchman,
Maurice Duclos—she's known him for years—long before you were married—in Italy.

FRED. Are you mad, Jane?

JANE. No—I'm terribly sane.

FRED. But you surely don't expect me to believe that
Julia would leave me suddenly without rhyme or reason?

JANE. She'd do anything! She hasn't a single scruple
or a pang of conscience anywhere—she'd lie, slander,
forge, thieve, murder, anything! She's a thorough out-
and-out bad lot—she's a—a— (*Bursts into violent tears.*)

FRED. Oh, pull yourself together, Jane, you're over-
wrought just because you've had a row with Julia—

JANE. Go away—go away—leave me alone.

FRED. You know perfectly well you like her better than
anyone else in the world, and always will.

JANE. Stop, Fred, stop!

FRED. She's probably feeling just as bad as you are
this very moment.

JANE. Not she, she's far too busy.

FRED. Jane, do please control yourself.

JANE. (*Making an effort.*) I came back—even before
going home—because I wanted to make up with her.
I've had a wretched night all by myself in a hotel in
Bayswater.

FRED. Why on earth Bayswater?

JANE. Because the taxi man took me there. Fred, Fred,
I'll tell you everything. It's awful. Julia and I were both
drunk, and before we were married we both had an affair
with the same man, and he's come to England, and we
were terrified we'd fall in love with him again, we worked

ourselves up and waited and after dinner Julia got grand, and ordered me out of the house, so I pretended I knew where he was and was going straight to him, and I went to the Granville Hotel, Bayswater.

FRED. Was he there?

JANE. Was he there?

FRED. Yes.

JANE. No, of course he wasn't.

FRED. Where is he then?

JANE. With Julia.

FRED. Ridiculous! I don't believe a word of it.

JANE. Nothing of the sort—here's his name and it's in capitals on the telephone block, and Saunders saw them go out together.

FRED. You say you both knew him in Italy before you were married?

JANE. Yes, Fred.

FRED. And you both—

JANE. Yes, Fred.

FRED. Oh, don't stand there and say "Yes, Fred"!

JANE. Well, it's true, Fred.

FRED. You appall me absolutely! Your dreadful matter-of-fact callousness—"Yes, Fred." Oh, my God!

JANE. Don't be so melodramatic.

FRED. Melodramatic! It's horrible—awful!

JANE. Fred, you were singing the song he used to sing us both when I came in—"Pour un peu d'amour."

FRED. I suppose you feel proud of yourself, having led Julia into this blackguard's clutches!

JANE. Led her! Ha, ha!—that's funny.

FRED. Yes, led her—deliberately. You've got a depraved mind.

JANE. And you are insufferable and pompous. Just because you like wallowing in quagmire yourself you think that everyone else likes wallowing in a quagmire.

FRED. Don't be ridiculous, Jane. You ought to be humble and ashamed instead of truculent.

JANE. Humble and ashamed! I suppose you expect me to believe you led a model life before marriage?

FRED. That's beside the point.

JANE. No, it isn't. If you had, Julia would never have married you. You'd have been far too dull.

FRED. (*Shocked.*) Jane!

JANE. Well, it's no use going on like that—it's just stupid—the great thing is what are you going to do now?

FRED. Do! I'm going to find Julia.

JANE. That'll be nice.

FRED. And you're coming with me.

JANE. Oh no, I'm not. I've seen quite enough of Julia to last me for the rest of my life.

FRED. (*Firmly.*) You're coming with me. (*He takes her arm.*)

JANE. Oh, Fred, you leave me alone.

FRED. Come on.

JANE. I can't go like this.

FRED. You'll have to.

JANE. (*Losing all control and bursting into hysterical tears.*) Let me go—how dare you pull me about. Fred, Fred, let me go at once—

FRED. I'm quite determined.

JANE. Oh! Help, help, help! (*They struggle for a moment.*)

(*Re-enter* JULIA *and* WILLY.)

JULIA. Fred!

WILLY. Jane!

FRED. Julia!

WILLY. Where have you been?

JANE. (*Aghast—slowly.*) So it was *you* who went out with Julia and not—

JULIA. (*Coldly.*) Good morning, Jane.

JANE. Julia—I've done something awful.

JULIA. (*Turning away.*) I'm not at all surprised.

FRED. (*To* WILLY.) How did you get up here?

WILLY. I left by the early train.

JANE. Julia, you must listen—I haven't been where

you thought—I've been all by myself at an hotel in Bayswater.

JULIA. What?

JANE. I came back here to find you and found Fred—
Saunders said she'd seen you go out with a man, and I
found that on the telephone block. (*She shows her telephone block.*)

JULIA. (*Under her breath.*) What are we to do now?
(*Loudly.*) Jane, I think it only fair for you to know that
I have told Willy everything.

JANE. Julia!

JULIA. Yes, everything.

JANE. And I've told Fred a good deal, too.

JULIA. Oh!

FRED. I want to get this cleared up, please. Willy,
what has Julia told you?

WILLY. About Jane and a snivelling Frenchman in
Venice.

JANE. (*To* JULIA.) Hypocrite!

WILLY. What's Jane told you?

FRED. About Julia and a Frenchman in Pisa.

JULIA. (*To* JANE.) Well, I'll never, never speak to you
again in all my life.

JANE. (*Hysterically.*) It's not true—we made it up—
it's all a joke—

FRED. She's lying. Julia, tell me the truth.

JULIA. Yes. Certainly I will—it's all a fuss about
nothing. Jane and I have been perfectly faithful to you
both—always.

WILLY. Before marriage?

JANE. Well, we couldn't be faithful to you before we
met you, could we?

FRED. (*Loudly.*) Is this Frenchman story true?

JULIA. Jane—Jane—forgive me, forgive me for everything. We've got to stand together now; they're both
going to be perfectly beastly.

JANE. All right. Willy, listen to me, I—

JULIA. Fred, you must listen—

SAUNDERS. (*Enters and announces.*) Monsieur Maurice Duclos. (*There is dead silence. Enter* MAURICE, *beautifully dressed, most attractive, and exceedingly amiable.* SAUNDERS *goes out.*)

MAURICE. (*Kissing* JULIA's *hand.*) Julia! Après sept ans—c'est emotionant!

JULIA. (*Snatching her hand away.*) Oh!

MAURICE. (*Kissing* JANE's *hand.*) Jane! Je suis enchanté—ravi—ma chere Jane.

JANE. (*Helplessly.*) Julia! Ha! Ha!

JULIA. (*Beginning to laugh.*) Oh, this is agony! Sheer agony—

JANE. (*With an effort.*) Willy, may I present Monsieur Duclos—my husband.

WILLY. (*Coldly.*) Good morning.

MAURICE. (*Puzzled.*) How do you do?

JULIA. (*Hysterically.*) Maurice—this is *my* husband.

MAURICE. (*Shaking* FRED's *hand warmly.*) How do you do? I had no idea—I haven't seen Julia for so long—

WILLY. (*Sharply.*) When did you last see Jane?

MAURICE. I beg your pardon?

JANE. Shut up, Willy.

JULIA. You speak English very well now.

MAURICE. Yes Seven years. It seems like yesterday.

(*There is an awful silence.*)

JANE. (*Conversationally.*) Do you think we've changed?

MAURICE. Oh, not at all. (*To* WILLY.) I met your wife abroad, years ago. It is so strange renewing old friendships.

WILLY. Damned strange.

JANE. Willy!

MAURICE. (*Raises his eyebrows slightly and looks at* JULIA, *who makes a meaning grimace at him. To* FRED.) My first day in London—and look at it—it's too bad.

FRED. I should like to have a little chat with you some time, Monsieur Duclos—there are several things I want explained.

MAURICE. I shall be charmed.

(*There is another awful silence.*)

WILLY. Look here, I can't stand this any longer! (*To* MAURICE.) Look here, you've arrived at a very opportune moment. We've just discovered—

MAURICE. What have you discovered? (*He gives a quick glance at* JULIA *and* JANE, *who look appealingly at him.* JANE *grimaces wildly.*)

JULIA. Maurice, let me explain. Our husbands have found out that you and Jane and I were very intimate friends in Italy seven years ago. They've only just this moment found out. I must apologize for their surly behaviour, but they're naturally rather upset.

MAURICE. (*Laughing.*) It has succeeded beyond your wildest dreams, hasn't it?

WILLY. What do you mean?

(JULIA *and* JANE *look at him blankly.*)

MAURICE. (*To* JULIA, *still laughing.*) It was cruel of you to ask me here this morning—without warning me—it was cruel of you. It would serve you right if I gave you away.

FRED. You needn't trouble, they've already done that for themselves.

MAURICE. (*To* JULIA.) Please, please, let me tell them the truth now—it places me in such an embarrassing position.

JULIA. (*Eagerly.*) Yes, Maurice—please, please—tell them the truth.

JANE. (*Mystified.*) I'm going mad!

JULIA. Be quiet, Jane.

WILLY. I'm afraid we already know the truth; there's nothing much more to be said.

MAURICE. Do you love your wife, monsieur?

WILLY. Mind your own business.

FRED. What do you mean? What are you getting at?

MAURICE. (*To* JULIA.) I have your permission to speak?

JULIA. Yes—yes.

MAURICE. Well, I am afraid it has all been rather what you would call a "put-up job."

WILLY. Put-up job?

MAURICE. Yes, you see I have known Jane and Julia for a very long while—we are great friends—they confide in me.

FRED. The hell they do!

MAURICE. It would make it much easier, monsieur, if you were not so angry. I give you my word there is nothing to worry about.

WILLY. I'm glad you think so—we have rather a different sense of values in England.

FRED. Hear, hear!

MAURICE. An obvious remark, monsieur, and not very much to the point.

FRED. And what is the point?

MAURICE. Had not the suspicion ever crossed your minds that here in England the husbands take their wives a little too much for granted sometimes?

WILLY. So they ought to.

MAURICE. It is a little dull for the wives. In France, of course, it is all arranged so differently—there are so many diversions.

FRED. What are you trying to say?

MAURICE. Perhaps Jane and Julia require a little more attention than you are prepared to give?

WILLY. Rubbish!

JANE. It isn't rubbish, is it, Julia?

JULIA. Certainly not.

MAURICE. You've been married for how long now? (JULIA *holds up five fingers behind* FRED's *back—unperceived.*) Five years, is it not?

FRED. What I want to know is whether this revolting story's true. Is it or isn't it?

MAURICE. But of course it isn't. We made a plan, Julia, Jane and myself—

WILLY. Damned impertinence.

MAURICE. (*Ignoring him.*) Well, you see, five years brings one to rather a critical matrimonial period as a rule. The first romance is over—everything seems slightly "gauche." Our plan was to rouse you up to a sense of your responsibilities—don't you see?

FRED. That was extremely kind of you.

JULIA. Don't go on being cross, Fred, it's all such ridiculous nonsense.

WILLY. I don't understand at all.

JULIA. We've muddled it so fearfully—or at least you did by coming home unexpectedly—it's taken all the wind out of our sails. Jane was going to break it to Fred that *I'd* run off with Maurice, and I was going to break it to Willy that *she'd* run off with Maurice—as it was you appeared much too early, before we were properly rehearsed. It's such supreme nonsense—please forgive us.

FRED. (*To* MAURICE.) How long have you been in England?

MAURICE. Three weeks.

FRED. Was this what you were hinting at yesterday morning when you said that you had a presentiment and that I didn't love you any more?

JULIA. Oh, no.

JANE. (*Laughing loudly.*) Yes, don't you see? She was paving the way, that's what she was doing.

JULIA. Shhh, Jane!

JANE. (*Hysterically.*) I shan't shh—it's all so stupid, and we were right, it's cleared the air—they were much too sure of us—much, much, much, much, much too—

JULIA. Will you have a drink, Maurice? Fred is still too flurried to be hospitable.

FRED. I'm sorry—it never struck me! Whiskey and soda?

MAURICE. No, thank you—I really only came down for a minute. I have the flat exactly above this one for a year.

JANE. Oh dear! Ha, ha, ha, ha, ha.

MAURICE. And Julia and Jane promised to help me choose an attractive cretonne for my curtains.

JULIA. Yes, we did, that's quite true. Pull yourself together, Jane.

MAURICE. (*To* WILLY.) Perhaps you'd all come up—it's a bit untidy at present—but you won't mind?

WILLY. No thanks—I've got to change.

MAURICE. They're sending for the patterns back at twelve o'clock.

JULIA. We'll come up now.

FRED. Look here, Julia, I—

JULIA. Would you rather I didn't, Fred?

FRED. No, no—well, perhaps it's all right. (*To* MAURICE.) Look, I must apologize to you for being so boorish. It was all very puzzling.

JULIA. Come on, Jane.

JANE. (*Still giggling.*) Oh dear—oh dear—

MAURICE. Will you all lunch with me today, it is so dull being alone.

WILLY. Thanks, but I think I—

FRED. Yes, it's very nice of you—we'd be delighted.

WILLY. Look here, I—

FRED. Shut up, Willy.

JULIA. (*Kissing* FRED.) You are a darling, Fred. Come along, Maurice; we won't be more than ten minutes, Fred darling, choosing the patterns.

JANE. Willy, don't be cross.

WILLY. But I don't quite see why—

JANE. Don't try to see any more—

WILLY. But—

JANE. No more buts—

WILLY. But *why* are you in evening dress?

JANE. (*Wildly.*) Yes! Well, it was all part of the plan, dear—you were to discover me dead drunk in the downstairs hall—we were going to rehearse this morning— (*Exits with* MAURICE *and* JULIA.)

FRED. (*Beginning to laugh.*) You know, it's damned funny—it really is—

WILLY. What?

FRED. The way we arrived and spoiled their little game.

WILLY. But look here, Fred—

FRED. Have a drink?

WILLY. All right.

FRED. (*Giving him a drink.*) You never know what Jane and Julia will do next when they start discussing analytically.

WILLY. It isn't what they'll do next—it's what they did last. Thanks.

FRED. I don't think he's at all a bad chap, that Frenchman.

WILLY. I wouldn't trust him an inch.

FRED. (*Laughing.*) The lies they told.

WILLY. You seem to have completely wiped it from your mind—the whole thing—

FRED. I never believed Jane from the first when she told me that lurid story about Italy.

WILLY. It seems very queer to me still.

FRED. Oh, dry up.

WILLY. But it does—even if they'd got away with their scheme—what good would it have done them?

FRED. Made us jealous.

WILLY. Don't be an abject fool, Fred. He was bluffing us—the whole damned thing's true from beginning to end—I'm sure of it.

FRED. Why?

WILLY. I've never seen Jane hysterical like that before—she must have been upset over something—

FRED. Are you serious?

WILLY. Yes, I am. Do you realize that we've let them both go up to his flat—alone?

FRED. (*Startled.*) Willy—I—

(*His speech is cut short by the sound of MUSIC above. They both listen. MAURICE'S VOICE can be plainly heard singing the last phrase of "Meme les*

Anges." He is singing it with great feeling—"Je t'aime—je t'aime—je t'aime." FRED *and* WILLY *gaze at one another with stricken faces.)*

CURTAIN

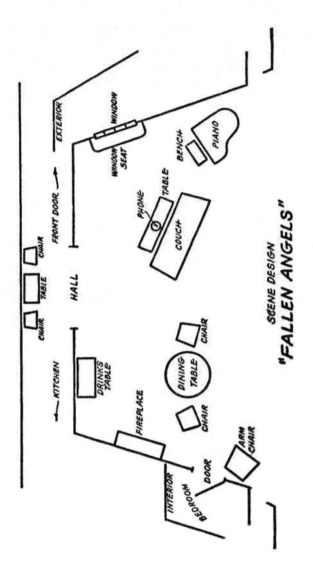

SCENE DESIGN
"FALLEN ANGELS"

EXTERIOR

WINDOW

WINDOW SEAT

FRONT DOOR

BENCH

PIANO

PHONE

TABLE

COUCH

CHAIR

TABLE

HALL

CHAIR

KITCHEN

DRINKS TABLE

DINING TABLE

CHAIR

FIREPLACE

CHAIR

ARM CHAIR

INTERIOR

BEDROOM

DOOR

FALLEN ANGELS

STORY OF THE PLAY

This is Noël Coward at his inimitable best, gay, debonair, infinitely sophisticated—this is Noël Coward in the style that won him his international reputation as the most successful purveyor of high comedy in the present-day theatre. The story is a frothy nothing, but treated as only Coward can, it provides a continuously amusing two hours, highlighted by recurring moments of insane hilarity. The plot centers on Julia and Jane, best friends and both happily married these five years. But before their marriages, both had had brief affairs with Maurice, French and a great charmer. Now Maurice is visiting London and has asked to see them both. Haply, the husbands are gone for a day of golf, and Julia and Jane nervously await Maurice's call. How they quarrel, make up, get high on champagne and quarrel again, what happens when Maurice finally arrives, very late, and the husbands return unexpectedly—these are some of the threads of the action. Another is provided by Saunders, Julia's new maid who has been absolutely everywhere and done absolutely everything. Probably only Coward could take such material and make it into the evening of sheer entertainment he has.

Also By
Noël Coward

Blithe Spirit
Cavalcade
Come into the Garden Maud
Conversation Piece
Cowardy Custard
Design For Living
Easy Virtue
Fallen Angels
Family Album
Fumed Oak
Hay Fever
I'll Leave It To You
Look After Lulu
The Marquise
Noel Coward In Two Keys
Nude With Violin
Peace In Our Time
Point Valaine
Present Laughter
Private Lives
Quadrille
Red Peppers
Relative Values
Shadow Play
Shadows Of The Evening
A Song At Twilight
Still Life
This Happy Breed
Tonight At 8:30
The Vortex
Waiting In The Wings
The Young Idea

Please visit our website **samuelfrench.com** for complete
descriptions and licensing information

OTHER TITLES AVAILABLE FROM SAMUEL FRENCH

RED PEPPERS
Noël Coward

Comedy / 4m, 2f / Interior

One of the "Tonight At 8:30" series produced in London and New York. Doing a song and dance act in a vaudeville theatre are George Pepper and his wife, Lily. They also have a genius for picking quarrels and insulting co workers. When the house musical director, Bert, comes to the dressing room to bum a cigarette and a beer, they chide him for accompanying them in the wrong tempo, call him a drunk, and oust him. Mr. Edwards, house manager, comes to defend Bert, and he is insulted. At the following show Bert had his revenge when he plays the accompaniment so fast the Peppers get frantic and finally fall down. Lily stalks off the stage after heaving her hat at Bert. Also published in Tonight at 8:30.

OTHER TITLES AVAILABLE FROM SAMUEL FRENCH

SHADOW PLAY
Noël Coward

Fantasy / 5m, 4f

One of the "Tonight At 8:30" series produced in London and New York. Victoria has just returned from the theatre where she saw a romantic musical. She quells a headache with three Anytal tablets just before her husband enters and announces divorce plans. Victoria, head buzzing, attempts to understand his reasons. She slips into a fantastic dream that reviews their meeting, courtship and marriage. Coming to, she clings to her husband and he reconsiders.

OTHER TITLES AVAILABLE FROM SAMUEL FRENCH

PRIVATE LIVES
Noël Coward

Comedy / 2m, 3f / 2 Interiors

Revived in 2002 by the Royal National Theatre in a production that sparkled on Broadway, Private Lives is one of the most sophisticated, entertaining plays ever written. Elyot and Amanda, once married and now honeymooning with new spouses at the same hotel, meet by chance, reignite the old spark and impulsively elope. After days of being reunited, they again find their fiery romance alternating between passions of love and anger. Their aggrieved spouses appear and a roundelay of affiliations ensues as the women first stick together, then apart, and new partnerships are formed. A uniquely humorous play boasting numerous successful Broadway runs boasting such as stars Coward himself, Laurence Olivier, Tallulah Bankhead, Gertrude Lawrence, Tammy Grimes, Richard Burton and Elizabeth Taylor.

"Gorgeous, dazzling, fantastically funny."
- The New York Times

"A gleaming and gleeful comedy."
- New York Post